goat song

by Dean Gessie

UnCollected Press

Cover Art:

Dean Gessie
goat song
adaptation of stock photography

Back Cover Portrait: **Photo by Julie Marchand**

Book Design by:

UnCollected Press
8320 Main Street, 2nd Floor
Ellicott City, MD 21043

For more books by UnCollected Press:
www.therawartreview.com

First Edition 2022
ISBN: 979-8-9867243-1-7

Table of Contents

this collection of poetry
is dedicated to my wife, Julie,

"just to be with you
is having the best day of my life"

Thank You
Dido

"[sic]stemic"

I take my black skin out for a walk
I dress it in all-weather livery
I collar and muzzle and leash

I bid my black skin do tricks for passers-by:
I command my black skin to beg and roll over
and to bark silently and crawl

I train my black skin to play dead at the end
of finger pistols or threat of the cage

I discipline my black skin when it stares into
the eyes of onlookers or when it snarls,
howls, shows its teeth or stands on two legs

I manage the triggers of my black skin's resistance:
I withdraw my affection and use the word *No*!
or I kettle and kennel with cordon and baton

I reward pee-greets, grinning and licking
with praise and treats and liberal petting

I take shit every day from my black skin
as a matter of civic and paternal duty

And I let my black skin exercise its freedom
within the chain-linked fence of black skin parks
and beneath the watchful eye of black skin owners

until one day bleeds into another and
(for the Juneteenth time) my black skin
presents its collar and muzzle and leash
and unconditional love

"diary of a dead eel boy"

at the wane of day my father and I would strike out
       small in tall rush and long shadow
greasy wellies and waders orange and blue through
       kloo-ik kloo-ik and *a-wick* and *a-wick*

my father and I would navigate fruiting bodies
       upright catkins and egg-shaped leaves
down to bat song air at crag point o' dark and
       the one twisted ash and succulent grasses

split the green curtain he did with his club-fingered
       hand and bid me break my slipping
gait with the sober refrain *care is the order* while
       hopping goat-like scree and rock chimney

at river's edge we left good altitude leaned one
       the other on sharp degrees waterward
and entered the lair of the eel down to the killing
       stone mucked with bone gut and gill

dark now darker on the face of father's eyes
       flint knives for sacrifice and organ dissection
he ran silence through nocturnal notes and brackish
       molecules blood spores in the nose

spillers he'd take and drive the stakes like a looney
       railman laying bed and ties into the sea
gather line and hook under foot and stab a worm
       fatway short to make show of the ends

out went the line and sinker straight points aft
       of entry and father and I bent crooked obtuse
and tautness in the hands that were the sign
       of a true lay or untold fears coal lorry black

behind him I stumbled hammering spare stakes
       tossing hooks and smelling and hearing blind
and always the *glup* of water and *kee-ik* of little owls
       and the dank of sulphur salt and nettle

through sand and heron shit we skittered palm-reading
           nylon and slack for hunger and urge
shoring up spillers and skirting carbon rust of hippo tusk
           and macaque jaw and dung beatle

and then he bade me do that thing that was holy
           of holies and life for life and seed for seed
but come the shot recoil and treadless boots
           come the slip fall and lumbar shock at sedge bar

and bubbling ho! and breathless hee! and gasp
           and pee and neck and ice and skin and smart
and entropy and amber trilobite and salt shad
           and mud fart and snot jelly and black hole

and father cursing the weight of the boy and sinkers
           of melted led and iron pipe and always
the hook and the mouth and the boy's leg for anchor
           and bloody minutes cut into his hands

until the earth gave way at the bottom of the world
           to the mud golem and the O-mouthed
oily thing wrapped long at his leg and father looking
           fire-eyed and hell-bent at eel and eel boy

and stomping spineless and clubbing paste-wise
           the jaw eyes and tooth plates in its ugly face
and returning next day with the sober refrain
           care is the order and spillers worms and hooks

"existential deer"

While trapping, hauling and binding,
lobstermen rescued a juvenile buck
floating head small into the briny large,
tossed spikes and legs aft of buoys and pots
and dropped him thirty minutes wide of plan
on the singing sands of Point Impossible,
whereupon the animal turned cheek with
desperate kicks and elk grunt rage and
barrelled again all-over good into black
eddies and white rips and aquaria lungs,
ass-bent on swimming dead right and clear
of those who trap and haul and bind.

"a mother mulls her son's self-injuries"

is that how it began?

the fishing hook in your finger
produced a scream and a sniffle
hung you to bleed out upside
down on your father's pointed
witness (a second barb on the
self-same hook):

don't be such a suck

or was it your brother's submission
holds that placed you in the court
of the grand inquisitor where you
suffered collosal clutch or camel
clutch and no offer of clemency for
a crying soul at the sporting end of
a bully pulpit?

man up, little 'bro

or was it auntie jilly who *popped a boob*
(her words not mine) and invited you
to fondle and squeeze through tears and
unassigned signs on a fluid roadway
whose solid yellow line produced two
directions and no passing?

only a pedobar wouldn't like these puppies

or was it the good summaritan two
doors down who touched you in your
jolly jumper or raised a tent pole
in your bunk while you pretended
to sleep on that lonely planet where
permafrost starts skin-level and
runs miles deep?

get on to walmart and I'll neighbour the boy

or were you cursed by the sorcery of
driveby tweets and snapchats (machine
gun shots of birdsong and schoolyard play)
when you were crowned *queer of the year*
by those who gender orienteer without
a moral compass?

nice tights, Robin - kapow! zok! whamm!

or were you a casuality of the anthropocene
a furry, feathered or ectothermic creature
sacrificed to timber, oil, plastic, oxycodone
backstage climate changes, toxic hand sanitizer
failed immunity masks or CGI micro-implants
right off the chip truck?

technology describes a boy that doesn't work yet

or were you mulling the fact that mom
kept mum as you lay prostrate on that
pre-op slab animal skin on your loins
moon in eye blood of thousands temple
torn and a stone scapel in your hand
to reverse cut the word *bitch* into your
abdomen?

is *that* how it began?

"gram bonkers makes a wireless connection"

Gram Bonkers had a stroke and never spoke another note
Doctors said she might remember come April, June or November
But she was mum as wood

Because sunny Rosie-Faye loved her gram like Fruit Loops jam
She couldn't say she was happy come what may
So, sunny Rosie-Faye gave her gram an iPad Pro

Gram Bonkers was over the moon to unpack and dabble
So much so that she forgot to Choose Language on her Apple
Instead, she let her finger make the rounds
of animals only she could hear on Amazon Animal Sounds

By April, Gram Bonkers had learned
to quack, croak and ruck like the Pink-headed Duck
and to hoot, chuckle, mew and coo like the Laughing Owl

By June, Gram Bonkers had learned
to grunt, honk and bellow like the Nigerian Pygmy Hippopotamus
and to screech and scratch like the Philippine Fruit Bat

And by November, Gram Bonkers had learned
to whuff-whuff and whistle like the Pig-footed Bandicoot
and to hiss and squeak like the Long-tailed Hopping Mouse

Gram Bonkers had a stroke and never spoke a human note
But she was esophageal-abled and Bluetooth enabled
And she would quack, hoot, honk, screech, whistle and squeak
So all the murdered animals would have their say on Google Play

And yet, sunny Rosie-Faye couldn't say she was happy come what may
Since Gram Bonkers learned a new language every day.

"The Burial"

at day's end, papa load pickle brine, the hebrew
      stone and grandma's bones in the sugar sack
and he say it honour his mama and the *messiach*
      to bury the word of one with flesh of the other

in my hand, he put the spirit shovel of greenstone
      and the pole of the thing that were my age long
and he say a boy would break ground where the
      thigh bones of giants raised the serpant mound

in long leaf pine, papa drag me wide clear of the
      devil's weed and what he call *zombie slumber*
and I crack shovel on hardwood and rouse the
      kee-aah kee-aah of woke raptor and *zizz* of thrush

by apple moon, the heat wear awful on the bag
      of grandma and she sweat out sticky spider spit
and ghost fog and white eggs and bits of voodoo
      hair and stink that were fart foam in the throat

down frenchman bend, papa kneel at the root of
      seven sister oak and he call out the souls of the
ten lost tribes of palestine and he say the prayer of
      reverence for tools, knots and eternal families

and he take up my greenstone and he strike the
      head of the diamond at my shin and we hear the
rattle of its kin but papa pull me high up like hog
      tripe and he say, *kill only that what god's due*

at indian way, we shortcut what were hallow to
      the ojibway and crush under foot arrowhead
and prayer feather and papa curse the heathen his
      idol pole and shaman mask and dance and drum

at manilamen swamp, I shoulder the bag of
      grandma and we wade cyprus and tupelo thru
nose hairs of methane bubbles and brackish spores
      and ear wing flicks of blood-sucking *maringouin*

8

two fathom long of plan, we lose foot in water
        celery and swim the boneyard of guineamen boats
and trapped *maroon* chained to plank bed and
        slave hold or dumped for gum sore and blood flux

and that when the bayou golem launch me star
        clear of day and grandma's bones and fart foam
and sugar sack and the hebrew stone weren't more
        than chum for the maw and gut of white gator

and go I under like john of jordan but papa jab
        me the pole of the thing that were my age long
and I ride the shovel to shore where he say matter
        of cold fact, *the beast shall swim the lake of fire*

by the *chu-chu-chillo* of nightjar, we find fairy
        foxglove where dug the ancient mound builders
and we breathe seed cloud of fever pox and spirit
        hunger and papa bid me piss round to mark claim

and he say *blond beards* and *atlanta* and *maya*
        were peoples of tall story root and poison fruit
and it were the prophet thru pharaoh that raised
        timber and stone in loam and elephant bone

and I dig ignorant of *what* and *why* with *how* and
        when fresh news swallowed like jonah at sea
but papa bid a pit long and deep as the shovel that
        were my age long and he say *jehova provide*

but the greenstone in papa's hands were some kind
        of riddle from our lord cause the horned owl call
who who and *who who* and I be damned to hear papa
        answer sober and true, *this is my son whom I love*

and I take on mud and the outsole of papa's boots
        and lay with pearl and worm and plate and grub
and the fierce *thrumph* of shovel and the prayer of
        reverence for tools, knots and eternal families

"#mentoo"

While on the road to sweet Magheramore
Hurroo Hurroo
A stick in the hand, a drop in the eye
A doleful fellow I did cry
Mary, I hardly knew ye

Where are yer legs that used to run?
Hurroo Hurroo
Where's the mouth that used to run
When ye went for to carry a gun?
Mary, I hardly knew ye

While on the road to sweet Magheramore
Hurroo Hurroo
We fellas pressed your hands, adieu, adieu
Some did cry boo-hoo, boo-hoo
Mary, I hardly knew ye

The army of tag-me-too, too
Hurroo Hurroo
Yuh stripped to yer arse and jabs, too
Swam with the mermaids two by two
Mary, I hardly knew ye

Yer boobs and bums in foam and loam
Hurroo Hurroo
Yuh swam with the gals to pox the lads
Plowed into the sea with blades and spades
Mary, I hardly knew ye

While on the road to sweet Magheramore
Hurroo Hurroo
Yuh made a briny soup of blood and bone
While we did eat clotted cream and scone
Mary I hardly knew ye

No, yuh'll never roll out yer bums again
Hurroo Hurroo
Yuh'll never roll out yer bums again
10

Yuh'll never take our sons again
Oh, Mary, we hardly knew ye

"old man seven bell"

     some cry, brother, for mask and screw,
[others, the powder and the finger,
     the pit, the pendulum or the judas chair];
how much does a child's heart weigh?
     [enough to bloody the scales of
justice with a butcher's bone hook]; I snuff
     with opposable thumbs [an ant or a fly
are the young ones] and I minister with
     an airless burlap bag [make a choking O
of feckless mouths caught between
     the infant's slap and scream and the bald
pate of a death rattle]; will you tell me,
     brother, you cut mean from mean?
[you who natterjack stone in the bowels
     of creation? you who command tons of ore
and a crematoria of bones and teeth?];
     fear is an eyeless kraken, brother, but
the tail will flail and have its victims
     [its sooty-faced and snotty-nosed diggers
flattened into pixels and johnny-caked
     by the naked hubris baked into DNA];
we only ask that they get off to bed by
     the seventh bell [so many more, so many
more bells before, to get the jig up and all
     fall down or call to clover red rover over];
is it abandonment you crave, brother?
     to leave your eldest all the righteous doors
while you suffer the closing walls and low
     roof? [you're no moko jumbie, brother; you've
not stomach enough for the cloudless legs];
     you never left the chains, the shit and the ship;
well, I leave you to your carnival shadows
     [and tin can, pot and pan kitchen jam]
whilst I harvest the children who drag
     their feet that way and piss terror this.

"terra australis incognita"

and Golden Grove and Borrowdale and Fishburn spat
seeds spirits ropes surgicals handcuffs leg irons
and fine English studs and joists for Government House
and those convicts had terms of 7 or 14 years
or the length of their unnatural natural lives
and among them that was cuffed and stocked
(and one of 172 females) was chapwoman Mary
what Clark called "damned whore" and "abandond wrech"
and those blackfellas believed these whitefellas
spirits of their ancestors (pale time travellers of everywhen)
and those blackfellas received venereal, opium, rum and pox
and they returned witchetty grubs, honey ants and fruit bats
and the whitefellas killed "no one" with their guns because
the new land was called Terra Nullius (land belonging to no one)
and it was fair to say that these whitefellas did not include
blackfellas nor irony in their census taking
and the captain struck the collarbone of the elder
(he that had helped himself to the whitefellas shovel)
and the aborigine elder embraced the captain and
spread his arm to indicate everything he could see
and the captain surrendered his shovel of wrought iron
just as blackfellas shared their axes of polished greenstone
and he was ashamed and he renounced himself of owning
and so it was with ropes and stakes and sacred land
these whitefellas pushed the blackfellas further from the sea
scattered burial totems of coral red basket and seagull feather
and there was bile and spleen between the groups
and the aborigine elder pushed the collarbone of the captain
and the captain knew it was wrong to survey and deed what
wasn't theirs and he was ashamed and he agreed that his voice
was no greater than the magpie or the blue winged kookaburra
and he negotiated to settle the interior space of Terra Nullius
(that ground that was less hospitable like them)
but the drive to fornicate was too great for some whitefellas
(chapwoman Mary said all the females chained for labour
were just "ready things for whippin and screwin")
but the aborigine elder petitioned the women of the blackfellas
and these women pushed the captain on his collarbone
and he knew it was wrong to turn a blind eye

and all those who rut without right were given an equal share
of child rearing with the men of the blackfellas
and handcuffs and leg irons fell from the "poors" and
"politicals" and these made a mountain of rusting metal
where everyone was free to piss but of the whitefellas
history and language the captain could not unlearn
the Coming of St. Augustine the Laws of William
the Conqueror the Magna Carta and the Bill of Rights
these were thorns in his brow and spears in his side
and he cast off his blue jacket white waistcoat and gold
buttons and travelled to be of them (even though some
blackfellas called him "warped from the form that nature gave")
but the captain humbled himself to learn "yellomundi" or
storyteller and "butbut" or heart and he was granted
initiation by they that met and decided he was 10 years old
and he was painted with red clay and fat of the wombat
and he received cuts to his chest arms shoulders and buttocks
and sand in each produced voluminous scars
and the penis of this whitefella was split with a stone knife and
a front tooth was knocked out to mark him as community
and he danced the tree lion climbing ripping and pulling
but laying in peace with brother and sister alike
and he sang the songlines that trek creation
and he blew didjerry didjerry through termite eucalyptus
pressed his lips to beeswax and shook out grins and guffaws
and the blackfellas did not call him apostle but he returned
his blind eye seeing to the white sails of Sirius of the Orion
and he stayed the cannons and six-pounder guns
and his voice was dreamtime and ancestral beings
and why it is that men and women walk upright
and those whitefellas that saw and heard were ashamed
and they pushed the collarbone one of the other
and they agreed against greed to call this place Terra
Australis Incognita or "must be there somewhere land"
and it remains so to this day

"the emancipation"

brother and I cud and mush *spit and chew* and
        gulp bitters of aniseed, clove and *crack babash*
and he costume *jab* molasses for devil *mas* and
        fork, biscuit drum and O-mirror for breastplate

and brother give me *dada* hair and stinking
        tot tots and *poom poom* to clear *maljoe* to *kongo*
and he fill me out dame lorraine pillows and
        jumbie umbrella and whisper *pay the devil his due*

salt foot in ox shit we stamp stinging *wowitch*
        and stunt *ratoon* in the burn of cane and snake
and still the *kaka-raka* of chacha-laca and
        herr-onk of blood guará and shriek of screamer

thru kudzu vine we crawl to the redwood of
        broke throat bone and brother eat the gut spill
of the dead ocelot with fly chatter and slug snot
        in the nose and headcap bird scat of *chitico cao*

round *oh, my god!* brother dose more *crack*
        babash and he drill *kaiso* and *canboulay* and
sing *sita eat di mango* and we make *coffle* line
        through master house and pee floors *mother sally*

at twenty water line brother leap red howler to
        the shoulders of *moko zumbi* and they stomp
leg holes through the roof of boiling and curing
        house and crush bourgeois slavers and *bagasse*

and then come the thump thump at auction
        square of tamboo bamboo and scream of *pa pa yo!*
and brother sing pole fights with boom or *foulé*
        or cutter and igbo bongo dance of *jagabat* sluts

but we mud faces and run hellway when
        Keshika's obeah say *not all teeth smile* and we
thirty of thousands flee the dogs at fever river and
        the *old french list* and cutlass and whip and stick

and brother and I skirt fer-de-lance flat heads
       and *duppy* unborn before I fall deep water down
at orinoco and spirit swamp and count end days
       in the cage and drown of white mangrove root

and my *dada* hair knots with sister of senegal
       heads from the door of no return and I see dame
lorraine in the O-mirror say *pay the devil his due*
       and brother's *jab* fork jab me and set blood free

"one big loud thing unheard"

I want to tell my wife I love her but
I have a red ball in my mouth
and fear correction
you can disambiguate the path of a red ball
spit or swallow
but the larynx is always out of its depth
never left the sea

I want to extract all those
teeth like shorn ewes in the Song of Solomon
replace them with faux sexy bridges
to elder care
I want to whack those singsong scrolls hung
like winking dirty laundry
until all the Hebrew consonants fall
thrust vowels
like candle-talk and hugs from behind
into the ghost red vellum of lamb
capillaries still bleating like stigmata
but my clam is a jealous clam
with a foot in the mud and
kidneys, a mouth, a stomach and an anus
not all made for festive performance and ode
Christ and his church we are not

I want to tell my wife I love her
with a shank of
cryptocrystalline flint
carve a hole in her abdomen
the size of Lake Texococo
retract the steaming guts
navigate a serrated edge
to the pumping station
and excavate my heart

from her
I want to worship
offal like an Aztec priest
use the pulmonary artery

like a shower head
sniff the adrenal glands
like a truffle hog
mulch the pancreas
like the Memphis king a hunka hunka
fried peanut butter bacon banana on rye
and then I want to launch
my heart like a comet
into the house of Smoking Mirror
where I, it, my wife and Pablo Neruda
will atone for walking like jaguars
and pounce on the
deadgod carrion
at the bottom
of the temple
steps

Or, I could poach synonyms for love
from a boneyard of vertebrates freshly dead
(no one's more earnest than a serial killer
with his trophies)
engineer my own Anthropocene Creed
from repurposed strands of genocide
I *eastern cougar* you
I *tule shrew* you
all I would need is a news feed algorithm
from Facebook
or an animal departures board
from Hartsfield–Jackson Atlanta
and appetite enough for wife, metaphor and
self-loathing

I want to wash my hands of
big flaming bags
of door-to-door butt farce
(the joke about your sister's arm fat
and the flabby folds of the bony-eared assfish)
(the fart at the job interview
I didn't want)
(the colour of my underwear
at the cancer biopsy)
and promote another vowel:

my tongue in your mouth
at the parent-teacher interview
you, a tongue wag of your own,
"So, how the heck did any son of *his* get a C in French?"

I want to vouchsafe my longsword is Jell-O
that I am an impotent chevalier beneath
the zero shadow of fresh wars on terror
that I cannot parry
a Shengzhou silk tie, an Eton dress shirt
and an explosive belt
that hellfire is an evangelical trope
or a wedding ring in Dante's *Inferno*
not a missile in Peshawar or Mogadishu
and that active shooter and live situation
are the new lexicon
of the Old Farmer's Almanac
horsemen as rapture-ready Kool-Aid
all blinkers and backstretch and in the money

from whither whence
when love is a blue egg
in winter soot?

I am absolutely disconsolate
in these moments of death porn immolation
(you'll be sorry when) parentheses
of hubris and remorse
because I have played heartsick next of kin
come to claim my own estranged remains
entertained worship that does not include her
and confectioned zombie climate models
from firestorms of virus and bad faith

it is always the one big loud thing unheard
and unforgiven

"the influencer"

when Radish Red posted online content,
we sheep licked our chops to click and feed;
she was apostle-gospel, heaven sent,
a multi-platformed, drop dead, five star read

and she knew when to friend or tag or ghost,
when to tell authentic stories to engage,
when to bump a placement or boost a post,
when to brand woolly flanks with love or rage

and she would Airbrush teeth in selfie light
or Facetune pixilated brows and lips
or Instagram faux face color day and night
or PicMonkey skinnier thighs and hips;

but Red blood in the tub no joy brought her
nor *like*-minded sheep *like*-led to slaughter.

THE PROPHECIES OF BEATRICE
CANTO 101: "The Virus"
From, *The Apocrypha of Dante Alighieri*

Byzantine were the caverns and the air thin
And progress for the pilgrim and her guide none
When Galilei threw light on monster and kin

And horrible was the beast's simulacrum
Thirty-nine times counted I corona eye
Novel agents of pig, rat, fowl and Kraken

And Galilei whispered hoarse "the end is nigh"
Unyoked cross and compass from his girdled waist
And left fireflies of spiral nuclei

And she who had spoken silent spring posthaste
Led me deeper to catacombs wet and rank
And bade me see things unholy and unchaste

Camel leg and dog, kangaroo and cat flank
And monkey and peacock parts in ample slew
And at each stop the cries of each my heart sank

And came I ancient medicinal to rue
And pitied I the beasts their hung cage and hook
And saw I gene and cell and genome and flu

And the prophetess lifted her burning book
Premonitions and admonitions unheard
And lit the way by measured meters once took

Whereupon the poet showed me beast and bird
Loved among one, the other and all like mind
And I drank fully of his grace and his word

And from the cave flew I freely and bat blind
The poet's *terza rima* like mammal flight
Each note echolocation for humankind

And we at rock's edge found both abyss and light
And one the other to steady leap and grounds
And antidote in what was good, mete and right.

"islands of mean[while]"

And Jonah's whale that did god's work spat them Muslims onto
Christmas Island and Jonah's whale mistook *asylum* for a
barbed wire hospice for insane folk and not that other thing of
shelter and *protection* since ghosted in social media
and these Muslims failed the *character test* administered by
the minister and they were given the seven keys of one-way
entry into seven concrete doors and these doors were shut up
words not unlike seven seals on the title deed of earth and it was
fair to say that incarceration or life less a day came as a revelation
and these seafarers ran aground among 501s or *extreme risk
individuals* (those convicts offshored from an island principally
known to import the same) and of these *boaties* one named FC
was thought to be a football hire until he overran his free
kick at the bottom of a cliff and if these Muslims hoped
to hop, climb, chill or chew with roo, koala, wombat or emu
they were best convert and walk on water like Christ because
Jonah's whale sang *no sanctuary for those travelling by boat*
which made sense since First Nations white folk had come to the
land of black squatters in the air-con cabins of British Airways
and he that was like a three-headed hound of hell called himself
No One and this bounce dog launched a beanbag round that put out
the eye of a Muslim fellow and this newly-minted cyclops reported
the dog fellow with his other eye seeing and Jonah's whale blew
a bush oyster of official inquiry whose principal embarrassments
were the laws of equity and common cause since no one
was arrested and no one saw a thing with the eye that was lost
and equity and common cause were fresh once again come
the summer solstice when those that were indefinite guests and
the dogs that guarded them tied off the barbed points of chain links
with wooden ornaments of bilbies and king parrots and waratah
flowers and bikinied santas and teams of roo singing White Wine
in the Sun like social justice warriors do and those that knew
immolation and rape and dismemberment and poverty and separation
sang with their captors *I really like Christmas Island / It's sentimental
I know* and Jonah's whale floated Pacific Solution for a kind
of Final Solution and not that other *pacific* meaning *peaceful
in character* and these boaties and similar cruisers of wanderlust
and bucket lists were swallowed again into the great belly of the fish
and spat onto amenable islands of mean(while) and into vinyl

subjunctive tents where they enjoyed various states of unreality
such as wish, possibility, judgment and actions not yet occurred
and these citizens of the Grand Unification Theory and sundry unsolved
problems in physics were once again wards of the Department of
Home Affairs henceforth underwriters of gulags and irony
and of those globetrotters, networkers and point collectors was a
clever group of Indo-Aryan speakers who managed to conflate
the rinse spin repeat of refugee whitewash with the dirty laundry of
ethnic cleansing and it was a great magic trick to do so since these
brown remains of pestle and mortar had already received the
watermarked Statement of Principles and glossy injunction to decorate
Top Side and State House with personal baggage from Christmas Island
even so, Jonah's whale was sore abused by octopi come ashore
squirting melanin from ink sacs (the same fifth column pigment
that makes human the colour of skin and hair) and these octopi
were incontinent because they leaked 2000 reports of abused
folk at Pleasant Island and the other all-inclusive locked up like
jumbucks in a tucker bag and one or more of these jumbucks
were diddled by swagmen and others were given temporary
mobility in 50 degree cells the better to practice walkabout and
one Muslim girl floundered like a dole bludger on a mattress and
she wrote in her notebook in pretty cursive, "I don't like it here" and
"I want DEATH" and "I need DEATH" because she had tired of
camp and character building games with life skills coaches but
her testimony failed to trump the *haute couture* of Shut Ins
these folk refused to be force-fed chips, spam fried rice and
cynicism and sewed their lips shut to indicate leading roles
in a horror movie in which those under the knife and under failing
anesthetic often scream unheard and Jonah's whale used its nostril
to funnel dissent into its own spiral air cage and those who would tweet
or whistle FC or cyclops or Raggedy Ann lips would be swallowed
into the black hole of the beast like crab krill light time kindness mercy
and the heavily redacted flight manifests of the Flying Kangaroo
which is why the best schools of fishes and flocks of birds eschew both
the human genome and Amazon warehouses in order to make poetry
with their fins and wings from well beyond the veil of tears

"what happens when I die?"

You will participate in an estate auction wherein the contents have moral and probative value and no one has the right to grandfather ownership.

We are the world
We are the children

You may purchase handguns for boys or crotchless panties for girls.

Having my baby
What a lovely way of saying
How much you love me

Or you may procure the blindfold of Lady Justice and use it for plea bargains and confidentiality agreements.

I turned around
She said, Hang the rich

Or you may buy nine billion land animals for factory farm slaughter and stream the scream of each through noise cancelling earbuds.

We had joy
We had fun
We had seasons in the sun

Or you may timeshare your brothers and sisters working in Amazon fulfillment centres.

Who let the dogs out?

Or you may purchase pharmaceutical industries because the cautionary principal [sic] has not spared the rod to save the child.

And everything under the sun is in tune
But the sun is eclipsed by the moon

Or you may option the rights to plantation songs that accompany cotton picking, cane cutting and rice fanning.

Heigh-ho, Heigh-ho
It's home from work we go

Or you may purchase Reapers, Predators and missiles and use these to fricassee wedding parties, schools, hospitals, markets, industries, cinemas, mosques, private homes, public toilets and lemonade stands.

And the rocket's red glare, the bombs bursting in air
Gave proof through the night that our flag was still there

Or you may refinance the Final Solution and flambé uncontacted peoples at a lower rate of interest.

Ob-la-di, ob-la-da, life goes on, bra!
La-la, how their life goes on

Or you may barcode human flesh for transport and sale.

Can't read my
Can't read my
No, he can't read my poker face

Or you may claim a fatberg of condoms, diapers and wet wipes.

And I think to myself
What a wonderful world

Or you may purchase toxic fuel or poetry.

Baseball, Hotdogs, Apple Pie and Chevrolet

Or you may employ an online troll to harangue social media users with clever asterisks – f*ck you, sh*tface

Every sperm is sacred
Every sperm is great

Or you may purchase life insurance bonds and mortgage securities and reap (grimly) the habitats and death rattles of those – like you – without opposable thumbs or blushing response.

You've got the brawn, I've got the brains
Let's make lots of money

Or you may purchase eight million metric tons of plastic, storm water drains and cruise ships with glass bottoms.

Wave babies, when they're lying on the sand
Wave babies and I want them in my hand

Or you may purchase online pornography 24/7 because free enterprise always finishes with a golden shower.

Can't you hear the music's pumpin' hard like I wish you would?
Now push it
Push it good

Or you may purchase coffee and pastry at a closed-loop drive-through and quickserve emissions and landfill to a squad of cheerleaders forming a human pyramid.

Ay oh, whey oh
Walk like an Egyptian

On you may sell pandemic masks at a 300% markup and come clean with hand sanitizer stored in vats of ghosted petroleum.

Love don't stop no wars, don't stop no cancer
It stops my heart.

Or you may terrorize black folk because their skin color and respiration create a kind of murderous, Pavlovian spiddle in the mouths of Five-O followed by pleas for calm, dialogue, reconciliation and replacement of sorrow songs with jubilees.

And I find it kind of funny
I find it kind of sad
The dreams in which I'm dying are the best I've ever had

But here's the thing:
your bid paddle is debt, credit
and bond. You *will* buy and
you *will* take moral ownership

of something.
Shiny happy people laughing
You may not crowdfund.
It's a small world after all
Despair is ontological.
I'm starting with the man in the mirror
Suicide will be your siren call.
With the lights out, it's less dangerous
Except, of course, you're already dead.
You can't always get what you want

Therefore, you will get what you deserve.

"tinnitus"

Okay, there's a huge armory of possible triggers and
you and you and you form a circular firing squad with
you in the middle [no one gets out alive or, worse, the
drum major keeps you on high alert and never says, *as
you were*]

But – who knew? - that five-alarm scream in your head
is actually the woodwind section of Ode to Joy or, at
the very least, a last minute stay of execution [you've
exchanged COVID or terminal cancer for an orange
jumpsuit and feeding tubes at Guantanomo Bay]

And your [upside] down time will be like one of
Dante's rings of hell where MMA fighters wrestle with
abstractions beyond their octagon of comfort:
existentialism and death of God theology and– oh, boy,
here's the biggie – the Interpersonal Theory of Suicide

So, what have you done to bring this upon yourself?

Have you been micro-dosing psychedelics to treat
depression or arthrisis? Have you been leaking
synovial fluid in the tempo mandibular joint? Have you
been harboring a super tanker of ear wax like the Ever
Given In the Suez Canal? Or are those pesky little hairs
in your inner ear bent out of shape just because you
used to listen on a loop to the deafening rounds of
"Girls Just Want To Have Fun"?

No matter, you've now got a tea kettle inside your head
- not one of those electric countertop models that, well,
turns itself off - no, you've got that stovetop clunker
from the attic, the one they used to call – god, help us
all – a *whistling kettle!*

And your husband's no help with his eagerness to
infantilize chronic suffering: "Mrs. Potts walked right
into your head. You know, that classic English teapot

from Beauty and Beast?" Of course, you know. She
was cursed, as are you.

And if your husband really wanted to help, he would
make love to you like a porn star, give you an hour in
the exercise yard far away from the solitary
confinement of high A above high C. But all he can
muster is the software of an egg timer, make of you
that version of Humpty Dumpty that all the king's
horses and all the king's men [and all the doctors] can't
put back together again.

At least, your son has the right idea. He's got you
listening to the Metal Massacre Series on Spotify.
Neither Mrs. Potts nor the Master of Whistles has a
chance against thrashcore and crust punk. Only the
rests in the music remind you that the absence of sound
is no longer a silent partner.

But you don't expect to return to the garden of Eden
any time soon [*as you were*]: nor will you be putting
your tail in your mouth and rolling east of the curse or
moulting phantom noise and running away on phantom
legs. No, this affliction ties you to the fallen world of
human suffering. You'll just have to shoulder the
memory of what's gone. And soldier on.

"american exceptionalism"

in wells-fargo
livery
the stagecoach
mounts a
perpendicular
drop
between
flat earth and
directionless
ether and
navigates
the step
between inferno
and frontier

a red horse
and a white
and a black
and a pale
shake loose
sulphurous manes
spit anti-matter
electrons lasered
rib-high
in fool's gold nuclei
and blow and snort
and pant and grunt
and pull
wooden wheels
through rock, rut
and tumbleweed

an eagle hovers
and draws
the shape
of the serpent's
tail in its mouth
to signal
wheeling

crop circles of
consumption
sewn with
calloused hands
and onanism

at the swing
station
in bowler hat
stampede string
wool trousers with
copper rivets and
rattle snake
cowboy boots
a selfie stick
emerges
from basket
and straps
extends
its spider-like limbs
into the dark web
and deploys
six shooters
to make the same
bulleted list and
slippery slope
argument as
billy the kid

> *the self-regarding eye*
> *of the storm god*
> *drifts from sea to sea*
> *in the amniotic radio*
> *waves of bluetooth*
> *just as clint eastwood*
> *eschews pasta from*
> *spaghetti westerns*
> *for an uncle Sammy*
> *hero on a bed of*
> *olympic onion rings*

through batwing doors

32

a wood burning stove
in a sod house
presages fire sale
capitalism
for can-can girls
performing
the devil's auction
in crotchless pantalets
to the furious rhythm of
the moulin rouge

(mr. selfie
goes on safari
joins the chorus line
for a screen
capture)

> *is that why america's*
> *first steam engine*
> *was called the tom thumb?*
> *to stick it to #metoo?*
>
> *is it no coincidence*
> *that thomas s(l)avery*
> *patented the first*
> *steam pump*
> *whose cylinder was*
> *digitized as a fist*
> *pump on pornhub?*

this version
of the wheel
and hub
grinds go-go
and kilojoules
of black
red and
brown blood
for soldiers
oil drillers
buffalo hunters
and mr. selfie

the first three
ogling
target rich
environments
at the center
of a jump
split or
cartwheel
and the last
snapping a silver
oxide negative
of the original
black site for
enhanced
interrogation

ergo
bruce wayne
as saviour
as batman
doesn't use
batwing doors
out of uniform
but bruce wayne
as anti-christ
as wealthy
industrialist
hangs folk upside
down by their bat
thumbs
the better to empty
their pockets
of silver dollars
and common sense

that's why
cowboy
management
reads
the stockholm
syndrome
by the dawn's

early light

to get closer
to god
we worship those
who kill us
with impunity

kapow! zok! whamm!

and there's plenty
of silver
and impunity
from soda to hock
at the faro table
where banker
and punter alike
employ trick
decks and
sleight of hand
and automatic
dealing boxes
to prove that
the old west is
the new jerusalem
and apple corp
its business model

that's why mr. selfie
docks most often
with the i-phone
the appearance
of good governance
requires arm's
length but there's
zero belief unless
you shoot yourself
repeatedly

hardly alien
to cheatin
and stealin

the gannymede
behind the bar
bears cups
to the gods
with fingers
that trap
liniment
in his hair and
gold dust
residue
the better
to wash
and weigh
incidental
commission at
night's end
his finest whisky
soaking client
and shoe
and snake head

the piano man
before
a self-playing
instrument
owns the keys
to heaven
because there's
no deception in
bankable notes

but his chicanery
plays second fiddle
to the banjo player
whose claw-hammer
style and drone
notes recall
caribbean slaves
whose new masters
are right wing
falconers trading
carrion for labor
36

and counting profits
in corkscrews
of chewing tobacco
or what you get
tied butt-naked
to an antebellum
tree or a cellphone
tower

> *is that why*
> *burt reynolds*
> *used a bow*
> *and arrow*
> *in Deliverance?*
> *was he trying*
> *to pierce both*
> *the heart*
> *and the hand*
> *saluting old glory?*

mr. selfie
confuses
pulled pork
with bear archery
sidles up to
the snake oil
salesman
whose elixir
features meth
coke
alcohol
and opium
and whose shill
in the barber's chair
swears
to resurrection
like the
pseudonymous
authors of
the gospels

> *big pharma's*

first pop-up
boutique
was a medicine
show featuring
a freak demo
ventriloquists
trick shots and
a fake doctor
that sang
like kaa
the snake

who knew that
kickapoo company
was full of crap
or that opioids
were rapture
ready Kool-Aid?

at the card table
their hands
winning smiles
the three witches
add homonyms
to the pot
the buffalo hunter
bets two
bison tongue
at 25 cents
a lick
the oilman
sells a stake
in his stolen
claim
and the soldier
puts skin
in the game
that is plains
indian red

this is what
you get when

you buy
fresh game
at a michelin
restaurant
(a hit and run
with oil-based
tires
roadkill
on butcher
paper
and a forensic
team whose
rallying cry
is the tomahawk
chop of
the atlanta
braves)

eisenhower
had it right
the eagle
will bomb
the shit
out of you
and send an
itemized list
with waxed
relief of the
great seal

is that why
mr. selfie chooses
infrared?
what, no light?

speaking of
gas-lighting
old uncle sam
aligns notches
in a wheel pack
drops the fence
into the gap

crawls from
the interior
of a safe house
attaches an IV drip
and nipple clips
and enters
the commons
on a cloud
of saw(buck) dust

      all and sundry
      hear trumpet blare
      and coming
      of the lord

      or so sing
      circuit
      preachers who
      see random
      noise as
      possible light
      and confuse
      potus for lotus

      nor is the love
      of yankee baseball
      an ignorant man's
      s(h)tick
      he steals signs
      everywhere

case in point
old uncle sam
must embrace
mr. selfie
at the knee
but each sees
eye to eye
when they hit
the matte
and lie in state

40

no one
overwinters
like the boll weevil
he's been spinning
yarn and sewing
apocalypse
since crossing
the rio grande

that's why
the first saloon
was little more
than rough
shelter
so jonbenét
ramsey
would know
what she was
getting into
at the business
end of a hail
mary pass

and it's mr. selfie's job
to make cowboy hash
of the legacy photo

he extends himself
through the roof
and into the night sky
becomes the lone eye
of persian magi
casts his gaze upon
the shining crown
of old uncle sam
and obscures
cloven tongue
and scale and dung

it is a portrait in infamy

"diary of the immortal jelly girl"

at first gush of blood, mama and I broke out hot
        in the cold light of blue mountain flies
through wing flick and leg comb, we cut foot
        and crown in pear paddle and burr thorn

mama and I erred hours short of practice through
        bone bruise, lung burn and possum grunt
and read whereabouts through *gleeeep* and *beeee*
        and tymbal rattle and *katy did, katy didn't*

down tall man grass, we split banana smell and
        hop and the jammy of fungus and curry bush
and I fell wide of lead over roo bones at shaman's
        creek and cursed fire sticks and lizard hunts

jaw grind come bog marsh, we filled toes with
        leeches at the swollen remains of fever tree
and called out *halloo* and *halloo* and laid smoking
        piss to signal our own claim and shadow

raised the stones mama did at bubble snail
        moss and mud for welly bits and shells for tits
and she bid me spit and bloody the totem at spirit
        level and breathe being into the O at face plate

and come the screech of the sooty owl, mama
        and I shed kits of dressing sack, panty and rag
and cut joints with the day at ankle and hip and
        knee and burst gum glands for weed dance

and mama mixed stock of fur eucalypt and
        wort milk and made antidote for unborn skin
and she whispered invite to the *ninety white*
        feelers and twisted medusa tails in my hair

at the sands of golem, we drank spores of seagrass,
        snake nursery and foul pink bellies of dead pilots
and fell to fours in the tracks of leatherbacks
        pulling clear of burial and egg bed at sea's edge

and mama's unbroken pearls of rune in uncovered
       moon were celebration of unconquered sisters
the words of scars no one hears when you wake
       screaming for opposable thumbs and kerosene

and fell we like fallow stones and five billion years
       toward the lair of tentacle, bell and stinging cell
and shrink and sink and eyeless seeing and blind gut
       and glory hole and *ah*! and *oh*! and immortal jelly

"familicus zoologicus"

unfurled tail and furry mouthed,
      a peacock spider hops leg to leg,
imitates hot disco funk
      and hunk hustle to win a mate;
courtship king, broggadacchio,
      one eighth-inch long, I, too, dance

pale, green-rumped, pocket parrots
      twittering shrill cartoonish tweets
reproduce imitation
      of cell alarms and app beepers;
our toddlers, capable mimics,
      chirp adult angst, *what the hell*?

red brown ant and fuzz bellied,
      hairy crazies by the millions
speak chemical idiom,
      jaw reflex and leg scraping;
teenagers, portmanteau for horny,
      leave pheromone in chat groups

a mystery, cows point themselves
      due north or south; unremarkable
ruminants, regurgitants,
      chewing machines and fertilizers;
you and I, magnetoreceptors,
      await late calls and take no shit

wobbling, dazed and confused,
      falling over, victim of nectar
fermentation, the drunk bee
      disorients brain and hive entry;
and grandpa, under the sober key
      of Herr Alzheimer, nazi guard

large ear flaps, long proboscis,
      sensitive skin and columnar legs,
the elephant carries great weight,
      joy and loss, human consorts;

equally, our lovely son's passing,
          the elephant in the room

louder than a sperm or beluga,
          the pistol shrimp produces gunshots
with its outsized claw and bubble
          temperature as hot as the sun;
grandmother, colitis sufferer,
          disarms with subsonic farts

fanned-out ribs, a dorsal shield,
          bodies like spikey satellite dishes,
the horned lizard defends itself,
          squirts eyefuls of blood platelets;
my daughter, sexting miscue victim,
          on her boyfriend rains venom

the clownfish, acrobatic
          entertainer, hermaphrodite,
acclimated for ocean current,
          perishes in captivity;
gender fluid, not like movie-land Nemo,
          our lovely son, dead sad clown

grey mottling, black baleen plates,
          the blue whale swims the Seychelles,
navigates a global slump in cargo shipping
          and punctuates freedom with aria;
locked within coronavirus,
          kareoki plumbs deep rifts

sand dweller, the pom-pom crab
          ferries stinging anemones,
panics predators, mops up protein,
          oxygenates its defenders;
you and I, symbiotic lovers,
          coordinate tumbling cheers

stout bodies, winter shut-ins,
          zero light cues in wood and mud,
beavers, monogonous engineers,
          build eco-systems; my dying parents,

45

keystone species in the biosphere,
       leave light and air in winter's wake

meerkat pups, parent tutored,
       eat scorpions, dead or dying,
the lesson, experiential,
       to avoid bestial venom;
our daughter, rape fantasy prey,
       unfriends networks or goes ghost

consuming mouthsfull of rock,
       weighting themselves for submersion,
sheltering from storm and enemy,
       crocodiles spend hours under water;
I, myself, clinically depressed,
       dark stones for ballast, risk drowning

sun-silver, side facing eyes,
       blowhole breather, muscular tail,
the dolphin elevates injured kin
       to surface air; likewise, my wife,
grief guru, echolocator,
       two fields of view, breathes for two

thick billed, robust and slender,
       holding grudges for transgessors,
the black crow pebbles traffic
       with nuts and gathers broken pieces;
my own case, grievance collector,
       I struggle to harvest mercy

sewer pipe, elephant schlong,
       forty inch long, six inches wide;
bladder-wise, three large trash bags
       flood the earth like mad thunder;
in the tub, my own urine geyser,
       no longer breaks the surface

cobalt blue, a spineless squid
       inserts its beak and short-most arm,
bloodies weeds and moonlit tides
       and fecundates oozing lesions;

no longer fertile luminous,
          we still enjoy bone-free play

my family, zodiac creatures,
          glow in the dark ceiling stickers,
less than the measure of gods,
          more than the sum of our parts,
caretakers of light and absence,
          loss of our son, the one black hole

"Deer [sic] Poetry Contest Judges"

one witness shy of a DUI you strike the buck in the
clear day of a nursery rhyme moon and douse its
wounds with Papst Blue Ribbon beer as you might
a dumpster fire

we see its lungs empty in autumn air
some kind of cuneiform language vaped into
darkness or a chat restriction or a death knell in
outer space

its legs twitch and strain like a single-player version
of Twister and come to rest like pick-up sticks for a
game of extraction from context

the deer's brindled hide fails at echolocation
becomes saran wrap over bloody chum or the
memory of that first drum in Mesopotamia
the prototype for phishing scams looking to cheat
the gods with fake invoices

you, too, want to cheat the gods
          with handshakes no more
          likely to hold than slipknots

the problem is this:
dead deer earn trophies from poetry contest judges
[a ram in the thicket is to the prophets
as a dead deer to poetry contest judges]
few tear up over gutsy displays from squirrels
or rabbits or blackbirds [poetry contest judges defer
to the heads of big game and mark their score cards
with crocodile tears]

but here's the thing:
you and poetry contest judges do not see the
megalodons or sauropods or elephant birds trading
human remains next to Denny's

you and poetry contest judges confuse animal parts
left and right of the I-90 for a one trick pony and
mistake a long game for a stall walk

too few
>   *poetry contest judges*
>   *are cutters*
>   *folk that*
>   *read wounds*
>   *with fingerprint*
>   *recognition*
>   *or trade blood*
>   *for saliva*
>   *like mosquito*
>   *carriers*
>   *of glass bits*
>   *of ancient fire*
>
>   *these poetry contest*
>   *judges toss*
>   *goat prizes*
>   *while logging into*
>   *Netflix*
>   *and tucking in*
>   *a burrito throw*

so, you haul the carcass into the bramble and check
the damage to your front grille
you might have become *woke* at this moment
[st. paul fallen from his horse and gorging on
chunks of steaming venison] or you might have
invited law enforcement [but you've got no
stomach for oxymoron] or you might have sat in
your truck and rued the fall backward into standard
time but you choose your own piss [end stop
punctuation between the murder scene and the one
witness you've already ghosted on social media]

truth is a fastball
>   *and everybody strikes out*
>   *on curves and knucklers*
>   *in the multiverse of REM*

most don't even get to swing
they're brushed back by purpose
pitches like flyovers and anthems

you pass out in the cab of your truck and you
remember how you never forced yourself on *that*
girl [dreams are dogwood whittled why-shape to
find water] how you entered her as a train the eye of
a needle but you felt and knew different once you
gave a name to that pseudonymous actor studying
the arts of penetration and representation at the knee
of Stanislavski [you called yourself *victim* and that
makeup you saw in the mirror made you a faux 'bro
of the Joker]

this is the real reason you fell
in love with method acting
hell, you'd share poppers with Joaquin Phoenix
if it meant your ass and clemency
were all one-way traffic

when you wake from memory you have a real
light bulb moment that puts the lie to those
who call you dimwitted

before you tuck in *Bambito* in the cargo bed
you rescue your Remington Sendero from the back
seat approach that 9-11 carcass in the bramble and
discharge one .30 calibre round into the high
shoulder and another into the heart because yankee
doodles are dandy when reading from the same
page of a high capacity magazine
        and those behind you in the drive through
at Burger King see nothing unto[word]

Judas, come home
        all is forgiven

the problem is this:

50

the guy at the window with your nuggets, soda and
apple turnover is a poetry contest judge who puts
the same price on eulogy and factory farmed meat
because chickens and fools wear coxcombs through
tragedy and comedy, alike

but here's the thing:
poetry contest judges will choose the warm
embrace of the serpent rather than wrestle
with God because they're only interested
in the kind of home-schooled carrion that eschews
truth for Whoppers [no one is hopping like a
monkey into the back of your cab with a stone knife
and appetite for organ grinding]

psychopaths covet the screaming of the lambs
            the rest of us fear what Santa knows
            and what could be more apple pie
            and stars and stripes and cluster bomb
            than a man carving a kill in his garage
            in the middle of the night?

you finish dressing the deer by popping out the anus
and pulling out the colon but you make a hash of
the actual decapitation [slit the throat, soil the cape
and blow your medal score with a short nose cut]

and then things get unsavoury:
the flood light goes out like a white dwarf and you
and your denims are ass-deep in carbon detonation
and blood and darkness and by the time your eyes
adjust they are no longer your eyes but those of
your kill [uv hot and virtually no blind spot] and
that carcass that you just gutted and beheaded has
morphed into that girl that you didn't force yourself
onto because of that Faustian deal you made with
Joachim Phoenix to seal the record and you recoil
in horror only long enough to gather up all that
Baconator and Quarter Pound King and toss it into
an oil drum with barbecue lighter fluid and a strike-
anywhere match

but here's the thing:
you've really ignited the worst case scenario
because poetry contest judges love to self-immolate
vicariously and re-appear in the imaginations of
those with EMG detectors or smudge pots of failed
taxidermy

your best move is to extinguish that funeral pyre of
guts and eyeball and antler crown and swallow the
charred remains of *that girl* before some bug-eyed
prophet batting clean-up in the multiverse starts
whacking fastballs out of the Milky Way and well
beyond the outstretched deer hide gloves of poetry
contest judges

"The Mask of God"

it is not so much *they* as *we*
who people the death pit, the
tomb, the mound and the ruin

how much does a child's heart
weigh? enough to bloody the
scales between obey and disobey

it is what those who sacrifice
do: make an ember of their
heart to be burned *ex officio*

I fill my sack with the souls of
babes and we in flame moult the
lie between skin and milky eye

at least, the gordion knot of sin
and atonement found its mystery
boon in a forward-looking Janus

or a pot of perfumed petals and
spices in a shithouse of asses; even
so, double-stranded DNA produce

in me the crushing cosmic force
of papa-sized opposable thumbs;
and how can I be other than the

pre-Christmas consonants of a
sheepherder? neither I nor rain nor
desert god is changling for nursery

there is no recourse, really, but to
don the mask, to look away from
myself as a black hole grey ersatz

the children give me example in
peas and shells and handy-dandy;
I will also feint and choose the O

a closed circle of falsities no less
hermetic than the serpent with tail
in its mouth; all the better to leave

the children in their beds with sugar
plums all a' dance in their heads and
the god of gog and magog a lap dog;

in my teeth, I clench the pearly bit
and secure the fit; I wear the mask
of humankind. *Oh*, I wear the mask!

"octopus in Grand Central Station"

the diagnosis is like gravity falling
you slide your weight against the hospital wall
it feels exactly like that bout of sunstroke
how you keeled over, arms flailing,
waking to snow blindness and avalanche burial

well, this is a shitty turn of events
the self-talk is a distancing device
salty language and toilet humour are
precursors to double-fisted road rage
Jesus, what are we going to do?

oh, boy, there's another hazard in the water
what you said after learning you couldn't have children
what you *will* say, sort of, in the last stage of his sickness
when he becomes both child and umbilical cord
Jesus, what am i going to do?

later, his wound opens like an evil flower
he conjugates pornographic locutions
to describe an imaginary *other* in perfect
parallel structure – grinding, contorting, lickin
how he never gave you the *real skinny*

but you've taken your vaccinations
you know he resents your perfect brain
trundles out tall tales of revenge porn
for his pseudonymous writers group of one
launches knives and arrows and darts
practices the black arts of near impalement

you catch as catch can as carnival queen
and suicide care-giver
busk your grief like a puppeteered prop
regale passersby with sobbing and convulsing
a hundred year rain event become
an all-seasonal affective disorder
your mouth a hat for ducats and gratuities
your body a caterpillar of advancing muscular sorrow

and you creep into the bedroom
like a dead thing or a battered woman
make a crucible and tomb of the rutting place
and compress beneath your weight the piles
of student papers you have neatly arranged there

of course, if you were sensible to human suffering
you might see the similarity between yourself
as de facto narrator of your own Greek goat song
and that greedily smoking, blood-letting heroine of
By Grand Central Station I Lay Down and Wept

but your lover has taken an octopus brain for his consort
lobes of mimicry, reflexive intimidation and inky camouflage
and you suffer blows as slow-motion oxidyzer for vacuum bombs
multiple aerosol clouds of shrieking shrapnel that penetrate the
the risibly soft conduits of memory and hope

to see it any other way would be *dementia*

"eulogy for empire"

South of Gomorrah
the ambulance enters a traffic circle
The wheels squeal the conundrum
of opposable thumbs
The Scream by Edvard Munch and
not a single moral compass
among the tire rims
Paramedics work the code
compress the heart and
oxygenate the brain
They are Yahweh and
non-binary pronoun
They will not rest after six days
They are cut from the same cloth
as those in Amazon
Fulfillment Centres
You are the fire and the remnant
wood ash from the year one million
shrunken toothless gene
from rotting rootless tubers

that they may know you
the already but not yet

The second time you die
you mount the painted wings and
giant rings of Puff the magic dragon
You see jugglers and stilt walkers
smell cotton candy and corndogs
press the soft sex between your thighs
against vertebrae ball and socket
grab the reptile's mane poll to withers
synchronize thrusts to hydraulic pistons
and receive penance in the afterward
from the preying hands of dirty old Uncle Rick
he of the neat trick with a dry hydrant
and a quick slide tool

so, Puff that mighty dragon sadly slipped into his cave

At Mercy's Own, you are jacked
four ways on radiation
and intracellular poisons
You can't speak
so you prophesy
become a tympanic structure
of scream and fart and
belch and stomach bubble
an influencer for the piles
of menopausal bones that litter
soiled linen and porcelain thrones
Veins of fool's gold run
the lengths of your arms
quicken like mercury
into your finger tips
and burrow into
the earth's core
Who will prospect and
sift your wisdom
when nuggets of gold
are sold with barbecue
sauce and a paper crown
at Burger King?

says the dragon, beware the spear

Outside the cicadas sing
day and night and day
They are town criers
with writs of execution
You imagine the thorax
and legs and head
in red coat, white breeches
and tricorne hat
The news is not good
from Black's Law
You will live a long life
and die ignobly
These bellmen have not come
to roll the final stone
and testify to resurrection
58

They troll and dox
with their cellular sex talk
and deep fake video of eggs
buried in glands and nodes
as much for parable
as procreation
You experience their
phantom vocal chords
as piano wire in the
blood flats of anal fissures
and periodontal gums
but their brief song
next to your jingle
has abdominal air
and three pairs the legs
It is they who will finish
with long sharp nostrums
planted in carbon remains

time for the sponge
says the nurse
and you are peeled
front and back
splayed and sprayed
and scrubbed
like old fruit beneath
a commercial wash
He runs a comb
over a largely bald pate
creates sterile rows
of psoriatic scabs
from a failed regimen
of apple cider vinegar
trims nose, brow
and ear hair
and deftly burps
the stoma bag
sutured to the pink
flower at colon's end

Anus, testicles, penis
and that abdomen hole

have become estranged
neighbours
or failing businesses
in commercially zoned land
or the four horsemen of faith,
obedience, humility and justice
or suits of cards
in a game of
diminishing returns

the Phoenician alphabet
is writing on the wall
you don't need bones
to read it
or tarot
or palmistry

What a curious decision
to finger each other
in the backhouse
only seconds removed
from skipping rope

strawberry shortcake
blueberry pie
who's gonna be
my lucky guy?

Did you take turns or
was there some kind of
Apple *syncing* going on?
some kind of apple
from the Garden of
Eden *sinking feeling*?
You wouldn't see Sam again
until crab leg and prime rib
at the Chinese buffet
the memory
of what you had done
become wadding
ball and powder
rammed into the breech

60

and made ready
You would only be hard
in your pants six
years after six year olds
had gotten jiggy
the imagination
the green shoulders of
the Kraken splitting
the green sea
of South Park toilet humor

you came into this world with coins on your eyelids
the better to buy passage into blindness and death

And you watch Pat Sajak spin The Wheel
of Fortune and Vanna White turn
the letters and you hear the cheers
of the studio audience and the cheers
of the slaveholders at NBC and CBS
and you don't know if these are
the same wheels and puzzles
that built the pyramids and dropped
a deuce of tons on precarious labour
the same wheels and puzzles
that gutted millions in Aztec temples
the same wheels and puzzles
that fitted black folk for fetters
the same wheels and puzzles
that felled buffalo and First Nations
the same wheels and puzzles
that launched Little Boy and Fat Man
the same wheels and puzzles
that produced numbers and
tattoos for kennelled Jews
and the same wheels and puzzles
that champion vulture capitalism and
Ted Talks and the kind of media penetration
that requires an exit interview and a rape kit
and you don't know that Pat Sajak
is a jealous god and that High Priestess
Vanna White has replaced the Wizard of Oz
the dress of one the curtain of the other

and that the *great reveal* is a wicker statue
that has no meaning in wind and fire
except to provide rest within lines of elegy

your imperfect epistemology
has been re-tweeted to satellites
in the jet streams of outer space
while prophets in their own
home are without honour and
the dragon remains in its cave
seated on its treasure hoard
asleep

Between fever and stupor
you dream of your all-inclusive
honeymoon in Cozumel
fall down the rabbit hole into
a skunk pool of Bear
Stearns exclusivity
It is unclear who looks
in the mirror
over your shoulder
your first wife or your boss or
a blind man who
uses his white cane
to tap out dits and dahs
and it is unclear
if he counts out human lives
lost to climate change or
the complete list of all genders
or the number of times
that pundits conflate the debates
and you, your wife, your boss and
the blind man share your meals
with cicadas the length of
small forwards in the NBA
share your bed, the hot tub
the swimming pool
the tennis court and
the massage tables
with creatures whose wings
are cloaks of invisibility

from Victoria's Secret

These exiles
from the land
of nymphomania
have come to score
defend and rebound
within four to six weeks
of full court press
You can draw only
one conclusion from
this steam bath
of sex and death
shuttered away
from the poverty
of frijoles
tortilla and coca cola:

LGBTQ is
the theory of everything
you didn't see coming

of course, Sam and Uncle Sam
were in bed together, too,
shared the same soviet Lada
while sexual orienteering
don't ask don't tell
and dirty old uncle Rick
had a hand in it, too
the brightness of his cheek
a thousand suns

is that why
you lost both your wives?

the kindness you withdrew
like a reversible mortgage?

the idea that you were
putting it in when you were
really just pulling it out?

have you always been a
jokey piece of Auden apocrypha
something that no one
would read
much less trust?

that's what happens when
you don a Guy Fawkes mask
and forego facial recognition

Later,
another dream coalesces
like shuffled image files
from vintage snuff video
You add to your maladies
Not Invented Here Syndrome
refuse to admit
that the horror of it
was workshopped
beneath the big top
at Abu Ghraib
and Guantanamo Bay
and Wounded Knee
and My Lai
and Andersonville Prison
and Kandahar
and Dachau
and No Gun Ri
and Haditha

oh, come on,
how many pop-ups
do I have to kill?

It was so much easier
to eliminate pixilated
targets using light pens
and joy sticks in
Florida or Virginia
your second wife said so
she a craven animal who
didn't murder for pleasure

or pollute her own shelter
or take a fist in the kisser
the better to see and count
fifty neatly rowed stars

she ghosted you after that
she made a ghost of your ass

Now you're getting your
phosphorous and your
asbestos mixed up
You burned
the flesh of innocents
with the first and amortized
cancer with the second
Is that irony or poetic justice
or the sharp edge of
Occam's razor?
Even the guards find work
after the war

hark in thine ear:
change places and
handy-dandy
the hours are the same

Anyway, you were just
burning tokens
at the arcade
airdropping that nasty
shit over Al-Sawad
what your own trade folk
called *plucking the goose*
because it's all white and
it's all like feathers

this one's a gut buster
the way you confuse
laissez-fair capitalism and
munitions that ignite
flesh and bone
Phosphorous ordinance

65

scorches the eyes of babies
and pillowcases of
goose feather
create a perfect snow globe
around the immolated
insulators of church, market
and hospital

Allahu Akbar

And who were your
own snow gods?
Your own perfectly held beliefs
in domes of antifreeze?
Did you kneel to General
Custer or Barnum and Bailey
Or Adam Smith or management
of the New England Patriots?

All that remains
in your mind's eye
are tropes of poetry:
Rhodesian ammunition chest rig
a pile of beard hair in a sink
helos and mike-mikes
one lone laptop whose screen
saver is a picture of white Jesus
and the crystal clear encryption
of WhatsApp (both the platform
of choice for launching an airstrike
and popular caption
for image macros):

now I am become Death
the Destroyer of Worlds

Otherwise sanitized
by the publicists at
CNN and FOX as
Warner Brothers
nanny corporatism
and the risible cartoon

violence of that erasable
Bugs Bunny:

WhatsApp, doc?

It seems the meals in this place
have gone into syndication
The turnip, the beef, the peas
and the tapioca hit the arrivals
board as announced
Says the steward,
we'll move dessert
up in the batting order
It matters little to you
which of the four bats
lead-off or clean-up
They all finish their
sentimental journey
in the stoma bag
like the Executive Branch
on the tree of good and evil
or the politics of Walt Disney

Dessert for the dead is not
at all like the austerity
you preached on the home front

how can you have any pudding
if you don't eat your meat?

Gifts given to your daughter were
wrapped in current events
and regifted to disadvantaged kids
You achieved respect and hatred
in a single kiss

like Judas

says wife number one,
it's not all about self-loathing

But you had no alliances

no Color to Go swatches
from the paint store
no pathway to game theory
no parade with the mayor
and justices of the peace
You were born well before
identity politics
and you long ago
recused yourself
from the social
function of language as
communicable disease
The Joker doesn't speak
for you and the Riddler
leaves no clues
Your points
of anthropological contact
are Batman fight words
in your neatly
clipped bowel:
swish! swoosh! thunk! and
plop!

It would all be so degrading
if not for America's Got Talent
You look into the deep fake
faces from Madame
Tussauds wax museum
and lift your hospital gown
to reveal a bubbling slurry
of leaking rotten egg
You play that hole as an
Australian didgeridoo
or a drone pipe
or the kind of trumpet
used to fell the walls
of the Fourth Estate
Each contraction of your
abdominal muscles
produces a burping
misty note from the
Star Spangled Banner

68

memory of revolution and
Rococo macaroni wigs
and real time septic sludge
that dots the stage
like the stool of Dali
and Mapplethorpe
and the judges immediately
stand and straighten with
hands over their hearts
and attend the end
of the HMS Terror
to send you and your stoma
directly to the Live Show in L.A.
and it's no small coincidence
that each presses
the Golden Buzzer
at the very moment
that Alfred E. Newman
presses the starting bell
at the New York
Stock Exchange
he of *what me worry?*
and painless dentistry
married in an instant
to Simon Cowell and
the stink of the
cutting room floor

lo, the spear
will have its day and

tonight, the cicadas are cruel
ministers of the black arts
The devil is their consort
and you the shining man
They will gore your daughter
as they have every day
for three thousand years
seat you in the ring and
compel you to witness
blood and dream of solstice

was there a measure of pride in her death?
was she not unlike Brad Pitt playing Achilles?
did not the javelin begin its flight as olive wood
on the slopes of Mount Cronion and finish
in the stadium of ancient Olympia?

But the cicadas favor fake
news and Facebook
algorithms
arrange themselves
into fighters
lancers and
sword pages
stage bull worship
from Mesopotamia and
kabuki from Kyoto
stand on hind legs
use wings as tunics
beaks as swords
make hand drums
of stomping feet and
spear the neck
to lower the head
and dampen the knees

the kill shot is that javelin
Sport's Day on South Field
an egregious impossibly
sick joke (you long for
cancel culture
and the end to
tasteless comedy)

By the fourth act
you will die
to continue the lie
or lie in state
with methadone, PTSD
and whatever
shiny thing
a flock of Jim Crows
has pinned
70

to your uniform

under the golden arches
you said
it's your choice, honey
book or toy?

the grief is too much
and not enough
our ancient brain conspires
to make us overeat

the dragon knows better
than to sacrifice
and pray
he sits on his
treasure hoard
all the livelong day
he will make no vows
and suffer no fools
with his tongue,
he eschews mythology
for the dank crevices
between his jewels

At night you would go to him
and he would hold
your tears in
his hands
ojalá
and his body was eucharist
and his own tears wine
ojalá
and he would listen to you
speak of Yolanda hour
after day
ojalá
and his hands made open
your ribs and he planted
there the eggs
of your
enemies

ojalá
and he drew out
the poison with
his mouth
ojalá
and his name was Sam
and he held you
through Strauss
and Leroux
ojalá
his love as great
as Yolanda's absence
ojalá

You are woken
by the exit
of one ghost and
the arrival of another
4B has stolen a scene
from *Airplane!* the movie
swallowed a rock of fentanyl
stuck his head in
a hangman's noose
and used a 3D gun
to blow brain matter
onto his NRA
Golden Eagles card

it takes a vet to euthanize a sick animal
that's the standing joke, isn't it?

The other ghost
is your own
There you are floating
just below the drop
ceiling
i-Phoning video
of the death
of the empire
and
the death
of the empire

72

of the senses
Your body looks like
a coat hanger
its sides and vertices
an empty vessel
the hooked head
a decimal point
for integer and
fractional bones

Still and all,
a lone mercenary
works the current
and the paddle and
the script like an
avenging Fury

the cicadas sing a coda
with their tailpieces
the dragon composes
a cautionary tale
each prepares you for
for the day when
all the world
will be carbon neutral

The third time you die
you float out and into
the night air to spectate
your own parting

The cicadas will ferry your
last minutes with their own

You and they will have
done with sex and
violence and blather
and food and psalm

strike up the orchestra
one last time
with tymbal organs

wing flicks and clicks
and stridulations

submit remains
to the ancient loom
and bid adieu
to the dumbshow
in the upper and
lower chamber and
in the holy see

It is the loudest song sung
in the insect world

Acknowledgements

[sic]stemic

WINNER of the Aesthetica Creative Writing Award, London, England, anthology publication, 2021

WINNER of the Ageless Authors International Poetry Contest, Texas, U.S.A., 2021

MEDALIST in the Nosside Prize 2020 Competition and published in the XXXV World Poetry Prize Anthology, Italy, 2021

HIGHLY COMMENDED in the Desmond Morton Internationl Poetry Contest, Ireland, 2021

FINALIST for the Plough International Poetry Prize, United Kingdom, 2021

SECOND PRIZE WINNER in the 90th Annual Writer's Digest Writing Competition, Cincinnati, Ohio, anthology publication, 2021

THIRD PRIZE WINNER, Mikrokosmos Poetry Contest, U.S.A. 2022

terra australis incognita

WINNER of the Enizagam International Poetry Contest and published in *Enizagam*, Oakland, California, 2019

WINNER of the UN-aligned Poetry Competition, Finland, 2021

COMMENDED POEM, Parkinson's Art Poet of the Year, England, 2022

Published in *poets meet politics*, Hungry Hill Writing, England, 2019

Published in *The Best 64 Poets of 2019* by Black Mountain Press, North Carolina

diary of a dead eel boy

WINNER of the Frank O'Hara Prize in Massachusetts for best contest submission, anthology publication in 2021

WINNER of the Spoon River Poetry Review Editors' Prize, Illinois, anthology publication, 2022

WINNER of the Allingham Arts Festival Poetry Competition, Ireland, 2021

HIGHLY COMMENDED in the Desmond Morton Internationl Poetry Contest, Ireland, 2021

TOP FOUR in the Oprelle Masters Poetry Competition, Pennsylvania, anthology publication, 2021

#mentoo

CONTEST WINNER and published in *The Best 64 Poets of 2018* by Black Mountain Press, 2019

one big loud thing unheard

WINNER of the Enizagam International Poetry Contest and published in *Enizagam*, Oakland, California, 2019

FINALIST and published in *Passionate Penholders*, Wingless Dreamer Chapbook, India, 2019

gram bonkers makes a wireless connection

CONTEST WINNER and published in *The Best 64 Poets of 2018* by Black Mountain Press, 2019

CONTEST WINNER and published in *Nature 20/20* by Willowdown Books, England, 2020

octopus in the room

WINNER of the Enizagam International Poetry Contest and published in *Enizagam*, Oakland, California, 2019

FINALIST in the Poets Meet Painters 2022 Competition and published in *Poets Meet Painters 2022*, Ireland, 2022

existential deer

COMMENDED POEM (top five of 2000) in the Magma Poetry Competition, London, England, 2019-2020

FINALIST for the Milton Kessler Memorial Prize for Poetry in New York and published in *Harpur Palate*, a literary journal, 2021

a mother mulls her son's self-injuries

HIGHLY COMMENDED in the Desmond Morton Internationl Poetry Contest, Ireland, 2021

Deer [sic] Poetry Contest Judges

SHORTLIST for the Aesthetica Creative Writing Award, London, England, anthology publication, 2020

What happens when I die?

Published by Cathexis Northwest Press, 2021

the influencer

WINNER of the Southern Shakespeare Company Sonnet Contest, Florida, 2022

old man seven bell

WINNER of the Indigo Open Poetry Prize, England, online publication, 2022

eulogy for empire

WINNER of the Samuel Washington Allen Prize for best long poem, NEPC, Massachusetts,   publication, 2022

Dean Gessie is an author and poet who has won dozens of international awards and prizes. Among other honors, Dean won the Aesthetica Creative Writing Award in England, the Allingham Arts Festival Poetry Competition in Ireland, the Samuel Washington Allen Prize in Massachusetts, the COP26 Poetry Competition in Scotland, the UN-aligned Poetry Contest in Finland and the Creators of Justice Literary Award [Fiction Category] from the International Human Rights Art Festival in New York. In addition, Dean won the Frank O'Hara Poetry Prize in Massachusetts, the Enizagam Poetry Contest in California, the Ageless Authors Poetry Contest in Texas, the Indigo Open Poetry Prize in England, the Spoon River Review Editors' Prize in Illinois and the Southern Shakespeare Company Sonnet Contest in Florida. Dean was also included in *The 64 Best Poets of 2018* and *2019* by Black Mountain Press in North Carolina. Elsewhere, Dean's short story collection – called *Anthropocene* - won an Eyelands Book Award in Greece and the Uncollected Press Prize in Maryland.

"Dean Gessie's scintillating *goat song* reveals a poet and writer at the height of his powers. Defying genre and canon, Gessie shapeshifts, skin shucks and shimmies in this masterfully crafted, explosively seditious, viscerally engaging magnum opus of satire. Equal parts alchemy, threnody and rebel gospel, *goat song* is a potent protest song to human, animal and planetary suffering. Threaded through with finely honed lyric, motif, imagery and metaphor, not a word is spare. This collection sings throughout with razor's edge wit and supremely slick syntax."

Anne Casey, poet and writer, winner of multiple international awards, including first prize in the American Writers Review Contest 2021 and winner of the 2021 iWoman Global Award in the field of literature.

Gessie's poems "torrent through the mind, an effort of resistance language like crashing a bus into a TV screen. Genius with a pocketful of broken fetters."

Tongo Eisen-Martin, from *Enizagam Literary Journal*, winner of an American Book Award, a California Book Award and shortlisted for the Griffin International Poetry Prize.

"Gessie's *goat song* reads like a whirlwind holding a machete. It takes no prisoners. He explores human failings and fragility as a Bacchanalian dance of visceral sensuality. There is so much to savour in this brilliant collection. *Eulogy for Empire* [the longest poem] is a tour de force."

Fawzia Kane, poet and educator, author of *Tantie Diablesse* by Waterloo Press and *Houses of the Dead* by Thamesis Publications.

www.ingramcontent.com/pod-product-compliance
Lightning Source LLC
Chambersburg PA
CBHW022038090426
42741CB00007B/1121